MACHINES ON THE MOVE
FIRE TRUCKS

by Natalie Deniston

TABLE OF CONTENTS

Words to Know............................2

Big and Red...............................3

Let's Review!.............................16

Index....................................16

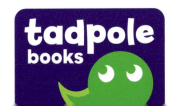

WORDS TO KNOW

firefighters

hose

ladder

lights

siren

water

BIG AND RED

I see a fire truck.

It drives fast.

light

I see lights.

siren

I hear a siren.

I see a ladder.

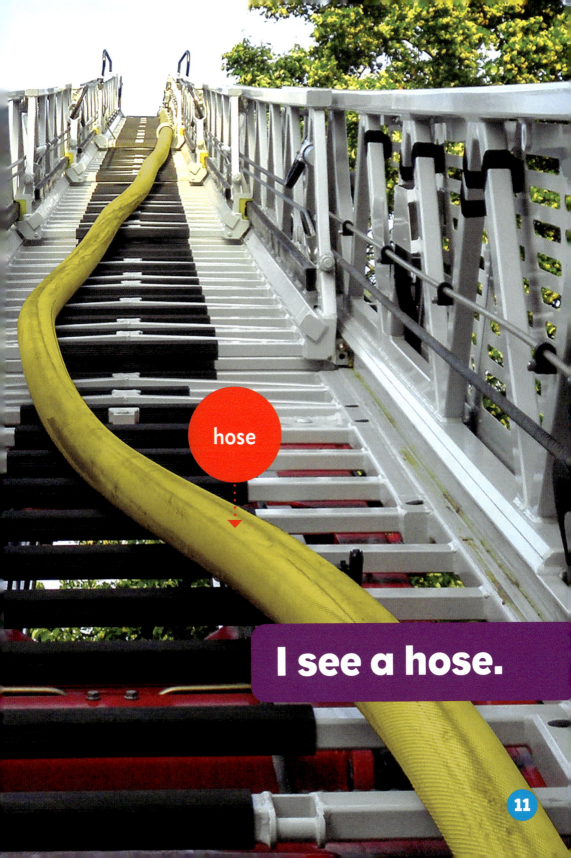

hose

I see a hose.

I see water.

14

I see firefighters!

LET'S REVIEW!

Fire trucks are big machines! What part is this?

INDEX

drives 5
fast 5
firefighters 15
hose 11

ladder 9
lights 6
siren 7
water 13